OTHER EDITIONS IN THIS SERIES

George Garrett, guest editor, *Best New Poets 2005*

Eric Pankey, guest editor, *Best New Poets 2006*

Natasha Trethewey, guest editor, *Best New Poets 2007*

Mark Strand, guest editor, *Best New Poets 2008*

Kim Addonizio, guest editor, *Best New Poets 2009*

Claudia Emerson, guest editor, *Best New Poets 2010*

D.A. Powell, guest editor, *Best New Poets 2011*

Matthew Dickman, guest editor, *Best New Poets 2012*

Brenda Shaughnessy, guest editor, *Best New Poets 2013*

Best NEW Poets

2014

50 Poems from Emerging Writers

Guest Editor Dorianne Laux

Series Editor Jazzy Danziger

"Art in America" from *Cold Comfort*, by Maggie Anderson © 1986. Reprinted by permission of
the University of Pittsburgh Press.

This book was published in cooperation with *Meridian* (readmeridian.org), Samovar Press, and
the University of Virginia Press.

For additional information, visit us at
bestnewpoets.org
twitter.com/BestNewPoets
facebook.com/BestNewPoets

Cover design by Atomicdust | atomicdust.com
Text set in Adobe Garamond Pro and Bodoni
Printed by Thomson-Shore, Dexter, Michigan

ISBN 13: 978-0-9766296-9-6
ISSN: 1554-7019

Contents

About *Best New Poets*

Welcome to *Best New Poets 2014*, our tenth installment of fifty poems from emerging writers. In *Best New Poets*, the term "emerging writer" is defined as someone who has yet to publish a book-length collection of poetry. The goal of *Best New Poets* is to provide special encouragement and recognition to new poets, the many writing programs they attend, and the magazines that publish their work.

From February to April of 2014, *Best New Poets* accepted nominations from writing programs and magazines in the United States and Canada. Each magazine and program could nominate two writers, each of whom would be granted a free submission. For a small reading fee, writers who had not received nominations could submit two poems as part of our open competition, which ran from April 5 to May 25. Eligible poems were either published after April 15, 2013 or unpublished.

In all, we received 1,850 submissions for a total of roughly 3,700 poems. Seven readers and the series editor blindly ranked these submissions, sending a few hundred selections to this year's guest editor, Dorianne Laux, who chose the final fifty poems.

Introduction

DORIANNE LAUX
September 2014, Eugene, Oregon

How to read so many wonderful poems by new poets, and choose just fifty for what has become the premiere anthology of emerging writers? One way is to fall asleep with them on your lap and wake with their images still fresh from dream, to go back and find those that linger like the last trembling of a struck bell. To have poems overflowing from boxes, poems on the couch, falling from the plush arm of the easy chair, set in neat piles on the flowered rug, a few petals peering between the stacks. To have all that, and be unable, or unwilling, to leave anything out.

I recently gave an interview to Kaveh Akbar of *Divedapper* on how I came to understand the importance of supporting small magazines and presses, to which, might be added, contests and prizes:

> *"When I was first coming into the world of poetry I saw how important it was that small magazines and presses accepted and supported my poetry, as well as the poetry of others I admired. Early on I worked with a small magazine as an editor and saw that it is really an occupation of the heart. Long hours, no pay, sitting on the floor in someone's living room behind a box of envelopes stuffed with poems looking for a reader. I also sat around tables in kitchens with a motley crew and helped bind chapbooks, by staple or needle and thread, hour after hour until they were all finished and stacked back to back in a box or slipped one by one into envelopes and addressed. Years later, I visited the offices of the* American Poetry Review *in Philadelphia. I imagined it would be a far cry from those small living*

rooms and kitchens, some shining palace of poetry, and I was so surprised to walk up a flight of worn stairs to a small office packed end to end with old issues stacked against the walls, books in every cubby hole, two desks shoved into a dark space in the corner, some sickly potted plant balanced on a ledge, under-watered, ill-fed, two guys in shirt sleeves, shuffling through envelopes on their desks, and propped on a stool, one ringing phone. It's all work of the heart...It's done for a love of the art."

It's a labor of love.

When the first announcements of the prizewinners went out over the internet via Facebook and Twitter, I was heartened by the responses from those who knew someone who had won. So many reposts and retweets resplendent with robust color photos and enthusiastic congratulations from peers, most of whom had entered and not won, but were profoundly happy for the friend or colleague who had. This is at the core of our small tribe, those of us who struggle to write just one line worthy of the world's blind eye, one stanza that sings, a poem that rises up and reaches out from the page, an ancestral love of the art itself and those who have managed, if only for a moment, to capture it. We rejoice, we celebrate, we exult and delight, knowing the success of one of us is the success of the art. I praise this generosity of spirit. I praise those who are included here, but even more, all who are not but are here in spirit, and in solidarity. This is not so much an accomplishment of individuals as it is a group accomplishment, each voice holding the other up, each one adding to the choir. I leave you with my congratulations, and a poem by Maggie Anderson.

ART IN AMERICA
Maggie Anderson

Three of us, two poets and one painter,
drive out into clear autumn weather

to gather in some harvest
from the roadside stands
where pumpkins are piled up
like huge orange marbles in the sun
and the gray Hubbard squash
are disguised as blue toy tops among
blueberries and jugs of apple cider.
We have to make our choices,
as in art, calculate the risk
of making them too ordinary, pale,
like a pool ball hit too thin
because we get afraid
when the table's so alive.
We also risk bravado
(too many pumpkins, or too large)
and, since nothing's ever free,
we might have to put things back.
But today, we think we'll
get it right because
we're not alone
and we're laughing,
arguing a bit,
examining the vegetables,
making up our minds, and
saying how we think we might
believe in the perfection
of communities of artists,
the common work among us.
What one of us does not get said,
the others will.

*The series editor wishes
to acknowledge*

Jeb Livingood

Julia Carino

Molly Damm

Teresa Kim

Mirabella Mitchell

Rebecca Perea-Kane

Jocelyn Sears

Safiya Sinclair

Jason Coleman

Emily Grandstaff

Atomicdust

Sara Gelston

Orbiter

"People make errors."
—*Tom Garvin, Jet Propulsion Laboratory Administrator
at NASA, September 30, 1999*

All day the world did not stop.
It was overcast. Dogs barked
at nothing. People complained
the leaves were not turning
as bright as they should. A woman
announced your death on the news,
your truck drawn from the water
by way of a crane, and I thought no,
not right, though it was in an instant
gone, the talk now larger, a passing
cold front, a man in Pennsylvania
killed by experimental gene therapy,
as well as the sharp rise of young
children killed by firearms from 1998,
which was an increase from 1997
and so on. I was no longer a child
so could understand the concept
of one thing being greater than another,
even when all things seemed equal
in their wrongness. I was not versed
in gene therapy but assumed any therapy
meant you lived in a house shrinking smaller
by the hour and were unable to find

the door. The day grew rapidly. NASA lost
its space orbiter because a team of engineers
used the metric system on one piece
and the Imperial system on another.
Before anyone could realize the error
it was gone, making a quick line for a region
they could all imagine but not follow.
Already I found the idea of such darkness
appealing. No talking. No mistakes.
No data on a screen to say *here I am, watch me*.
In Japan, it was already the next morning.
It was autumn there too, though fewer people
made a thing of it. A man in a hard hat
downplayed the evacuation of 80,000 people
surrounding the Tokaimura nuclear plant.
It looked overcast, though it was difficult
to say from what. The translation beneath
him read *not Chernobyl*, which to me meant
the placing of not in front of any tragedy
might undo the tragedy itself. All day people
went from one thing to the next, unaware
of the levels of loss that all had to be calculated,
weighed against these perfect errors of absence.
I could hardly believe it. Not drowned,
I practiced but could not bring myself to say.
Not right. What circles the sun and is never found.

Nico Alvarado

Tim Riggins Speaks of Waterfalls

You want to know what it was like?
It was like my whole life had a fever.
Whole acres of me were on fire.
The sun talked dirty in my ear all night.
I couldn't drive past a wheatfield without doing it violence.
I couldn't even look at a bridge.
I used to go out in the brush sometimes,
So far out there no one could hear me,
And just burn.
I felt all right then.
I couldn't hurt anyone else.
I was just a pillar of fire.
It wasn't the burning so much as the loneliness.
It wasn't the loneliness so much as the fear of being alone.
Christ look at you pouring from the rocks.
You're so cold you're boiling over.
You've got stars in your hair.
I don't want to be around you.
I don't want to drink you in.
I want to walk into the heart of you
And never walk back out.

NOMINATED BY *GULF COAST*

Phillip B. Williams

Do-rag

O darling, the moon did not disrobe you.
You fell asleep that way, nude
and capsized by our wine, our Bump

'N Grind shenanigans. Blame it
on whatever you like; my bed welcomes
whomever you decide to be: thug-

mistress, poinsettia, John Doe
in the alcove of my dreams. You
can quote verbatim an entire album

of Bone Thugs-N-Harmony
with your ass in the air. There's nothing
wrong with that. They mince syllables

as you call me yours. You don't
like me but still invite me to your home
when your homies aren't near

enough to hear us crash into each other
like hours. Some men have killed
their lovers because they loved them

so much in secret that the secret kept
coming out: wife gouging her husband
with suspicion, churches sneering

when an usher enters. Never mind that.
The sickle moon turns the sky into
a man's mouth slapped sideways

to keep him from spilling what no one would
understand: you call me God when it
gets good though I do not exist to you

outside this room. Be yourself or no one else
here. Your do-rag is camouflage-patterned
and stuffed into my mouth.

Miriam Bird Greenberg

Shortness of Breath

The kind of animal
who comes in from the woods
to a town with only two
telephones and presses
the mass of his enormous body
against the glass face
of the telephone exchange,
where someone working
late, or expecting
a call, might see it
on hind legs
fill the window
like a shortness of breath,
brief interruption of fur
from scars running
across its chest—
then retreat into the enormous
night. It is this kind
of animal I once spoke
to, unarmed, approaching
a rock ledge where the stone
parted and was filled
by air—then the air
parted, and what remained
there was only the fearful

unknown,
which we both smelled
on the wind.

NOMINATED BY THE *Paris-American*

Joy Priest
Nightstick

in Kentucky you are a Black girl, but don't know. you sleep
next to it. crooked bone, split-open head. patrolling through the night.
don't even know you should be trying to run away. it rests
in your night terrors, in a bureau between your grandmother's quilts,
with her thimbles & thread & dead white poems. don't think
for a moment your grandfather won't pull it out, make a cross of it
with your arms, gift you its weight & crime. do you believe?
what if he said its name was *Justice*? would that be too much?
if he was the only man your childhood saw hauled away in handcuffs,
pale & liver-spotted & stiff in limbs sharp enough to fold into the back
of a cruiser? you. this bruise of irony. the only two Blacks ever allowed
in his house. & at night he be singing you to sleep while it sits invisible,
sentry-like out of sight. he be humming hymns—*i come to the garden*
alone while the dew is still on the roses—knowing how much blood it's seen &
whose. he be holding you to himself like a secret & every song be a prayer
for your daddy's sunk-in head. you breathing one for his whole face
before you. bullying a shit-shaded boy's head is what it's made for,
he say, your papaw, while you hold it, not knowing enough about yourself
to understand the cannibal nature of chewing on these words with no riot
inside. no baton twirling in the air of your stomach. no notice of the grand
wizard & his wand when he appears in your nightmare. you be closed-eye
& it be there, Black as who it means to beat

C.L. O'Dell
My Father Named the Trees

and I listened, in a swamp full of wild grapes
grouse hid in shoes of clover, bowls of winter wheat.
You named the trees so there were trees with names
only we knew. Our guns softly touched their bark,
barrels quiet white with failure. It was morning.
You set silence before me like shallow seeds,
led me into disappearance; buckshot like piano keys
in my pocket. And the slags of boyhood would ghost,
glaze my eyes, like the spots of a fawn sink
inside them, and stay there, and promise.

Ellie Sawatzky

Repeat Offenders

April '83, two months out of med school, deep in debt,
he goes North. Ties a string to Irene's finger, promising

to write. Soft tundra under the overnight train. Yellow
moon in the shape of an earlobe. Churchill—

packed snow squeaks like styrofoam, beer is cheaper
than milk. You keep warm with whiskey, the blue fire

of cable TV. No roads to speak of. Grain comes by train
from the prairies, ships to Europe. Sea crews

from Murmansk, Jakarta. In the hospital he treats parasites
as often as frostbite. Flirts with nurses who knit sweaters

from dog fur. Mornings, he jogs on the shore. He writes
to Irene, leaves out the flirting, tells her

Winnipeg's got nothing on this rough season, and he misses
trees. Tells her he delivered a baby in an airplane,

and it's almost true—he was there. Hudson's Bay
breakup waits 'til July. The doctors windsurf between

ice floes, sipping martinis from IV bags. Narwhals
in the mouth of the river. Thanksgiving—

frozen grapes 'round the turkey. It's bear season.
Irene wants to know if he's seen them—

he has. Pacing the shoreline for seals. Circling
the outskirts of town at Hallowe'en, doing their best

trick-or-treat. He's seen them in bear jail, repeat offenders,
numbers spraypainted in black on their sides. Seen them

for sale on the banks of Coral Harbour, pelts gone slack,
more yellow than white, strung up to dry in the sun.

Christmas, he drives five miles south to find a tree, decorates
with barnacles, fish hooks. Drinks rum with powdered eggnog,

frequents the bar, spends night after night with nurses,
an animal trying to stay warm. In the dry heart of winter,

the hotel burns down. Days later, a man from town roots
for liquor in the black rubble, doesn't see the light

shift, the shadow of the bear. He writes to Irene, tells her
how the man bled out on his table, thin strings of sinew holding

his head to his body. And what he looked like then—
skin gone slack and sallow, more yellow than white.

NOMINATED BY THE UNIVERSITY OF BRITISH COLUMBIA CREATIVE WRITING PROGRAM

Matthew Minicucci
A Whale's Heart

There's a sadness that smells
      like rose water. It's my father's

hands on the receiver, his voice, how his own
      father just can't find the words

anymore. *If you give him time*, he says, like a slow
      climb, the single-stroke engine sputtering, spilling

oil; falling behind. *When you're deaf, sometimes
      you just stop* listening; I understand, how

sometimes it snows inside the skull; how much
      like wind, like nothing. How lovely these

fingerless gloves sewn; how inevitable. My
      grandfather once said you can hear

a whale's heart from over two miles
      away. How much sound must dissipate

through the wavering quiet; the medium. How
      large the ventricles must be.

How, in the old country, his family distilled
      the petals pulled from their rose

garden. As drink, or drug, or perfume
        applied to his own father's ears each

night, before prayers; how the burns came
        in a blacksmith's fire; how small the scar

left, how easy to see then
        what was lost.

Ocean Vuong
Anaphora as Coping Mechanism

Can't sleep
so you put on his grey boots—nothing else—and step out
in the rain. *Even though he's dead* you think, *I still want
to be clean.* If only the rain was gasoline, your tongue
a lit match. If only he dies the second his name
becomes a tooth in your mouth. But he doesn't. He dies
when his heart stops and heat retreats to its bluer shades, blood
pooled where it last bursted, slack like rain in a pothole. He dies
when they wheel him away and the priest ushers you out of the room,
your face darkening behind your hands. He dies as your heart beats
faster, your palms two puddles of rain. He dies each night
you close your eyes and hear his slow exhale. Your hand choking
the dark. Your hand through the bathroom mirror just to see yourself
in multitudes. He dies at the party where everyone laughs
and all you want to do is go into the kitchen and make seven omelets
before burning down the house. All you want is to run into the woods
and beg the wolf to fuck you up. He dies as soon as you wake up
and it's November for months. The coffee like salt water. The song
on the record stuck on *please.* He dies the morning he kisses you
for two minutes too long, when he says *I love you* followed by
I have something to say and you quickly grab your favorite pink pillow
and smother him as he cries into the soft and darkening fabric.
You hold very still as you look out the window, at the streak
of ochre light smeared on the young birch. And you breathe.
You breathe thinking of summer, the long evenings pressed
into smoke-soaked skin. You hold still until he's very quiet,

until the room fades black and you're both standing
in the crowded train again. You're leaning back
into his chest and he doesn't know your name yet, but he doesn't
move. You're letting go of the pole now. You feel his breaths
on your neck and smile for the first time in weeks. And he just
stands there with his eyes closed, the back of your head nestled
in his sternum. He doesn't know your name yet. The train
rocks you back and forth like a slow dance you watch
from the distance of years. His dimples reflected
in the window reflecting your lips as you mouth the words
thank you. Your tongue a lit match.

NOMINATED BY THE *SOUTHERN INDIANA REVIEW*

Talin Tahajian
The river burns /
Armenia, 1915

does not burn / how many bullets would it take / I have never held a gun / I have / bodies that turn to birds / flicker against smoke / we are not dead yet / winter is the most insatiable season / said your grandmother / before she disappeared into the smoke / flickering birds / I am learning / to misread signs / *if you fill my canteen with water* / *I will introduce you to my beautiful sister* / they married / we remember / April for all its wild roses / have you noticed / they bloom as the river burns / there is no fire / only water / I was named after a village / not a person / but what good is it to know places / *I have travelled across deserts* / perhaps this is why we speak of burning / desert nights / there is nothing that smells so much like bone / I understand / why we speak of burning / even when there is no fire / why we have names / what was the desert / the river / the thin-lipped moon / the girl beneath all that burning / skin

Linda Blaskey

Looking West Toward the Ozarks

My bones are losing calcium.

This is how it will end I think—
bones thinning to chalk—

      Chalk is calcium carbonate.

On the sandstone bluffs above the Buffalo River
I will use chalk to write my life in glyphs—
      one for mountain
      one for father
      one for hearth
      one for leaving

This is how it will end I think—
the rain will finally come,
words from bone will wash away.

My sons will lose the path home.

Kate Angus
Wild Rabbits Have Sharp Eyes

Which is another way of saying, *everything you want to hide*
blares like a motel's Vacant sign. How long it took

for you to tumble into sleeping on the couch, the bed stripped
except for piles of laundry you could not bring yourself

to put away. Do you remember when you didn't
live inside this city's constant siren, when you were

the teenager in the woods, wearing dark like a blanket, the night
studded with stars as many as your friends. It's just the past now:

the teenagers you later taught are all adults now.
They have children, lovers. You have a certain archive of a mind

that files away the beautiful impractical. For example: *The Amish*
cultivate saffron. For example, *Octopi have three hearts and die*

of starvation—the mothers stop eating while they guard
their unhatched eggs. So you know things.

Knowledge doesn't fix the faucet whose drip stains
the white sink chlorine blue. Information is only your own hands

stroking your hips as you turn each night. What you would give
to be a wheat field during a storm. Stalks bending, seeded

by violent rain, and the sky a clotted
purple arch above you, lightning strikes that jolt you so you remember

no matter how dead you feel you are not dead.

Peter LaBerge

Peter

Drexel University, February 2014.

In my mind the foliate scrolls dangle,
beer-soaked, from the ceiling.

I have named you Peter because he was the first
apostle to learn the journey, to chart
each hill of me.

*

Night stains the bookshelves. The moon,
white and swallowed.

A floor buckling to the ceiling, my throat.
The moon from you to my mouth.

*

My shoulders melting,
wickless, into this dish of skin.

My shoulders gleaming
through a slit as wide as a post slot.

*

I don't know how to say I've never tasted
the inside of someone else.

I don't know how to say our blessed name.

Noel Crook

Notes from a Salt Flat Prisoner

Bonaire

On this island, love, there is nothing but black
and white—the sea's flat back that keeps us,
bleak shards of coral honed sharp as knives
by tireless wavelets. And the salt—vast,
blinding pans for us to rake. It galls
our wrists and shins like manacles.

Nothing grows here but these crystals. Even
the dark seaweed swirling in the inlets
rises on spindly legs as if to swim
away. Small black lizards whisper
names of home against the dry rocks
and we boil them for it. We are sick

of fish. All day the sun's blanched eye
seeks us, and not one rock
big enough to hide under. I am changed
by this place—like Lot's wife
I look back, reconfigure
the purple shadows in the struts of your

ribs, your tongue in my mouth like pure fire.
Here there is no holy water or sin.
Each night we bathe ourselves in brine,

lie under a black collar of sky, the spume
of white salt stars, the salt white moon,
the sting of crystals blooming on our skin.

NOMINATED BY *Smartish Pace*

Rachel Morgenstern-Clarren
The Civil War Photographer

In my portrait studio, I place each
soldier's head between a metal vise

to keep him still. But things move
too fast in the field.

I photograph what remains
after the fighting's done: not smoke

but the cold cannon, the burnt-
out mill, the singed hills. Branches

curling inward like a man's nails
grown wild. I wish I had the speed

& color to capture
the ceasefire, when soldiers

on both sides go blackberrying.
The chaos of their arms

plunging into the gaps,
skin brambling to a blackish-red,

mouths bursting from juice & thorns.
How they hurt for what sustains them.

Anna Rose Welch

La Petite Mort

Affection had nothing to do with it.

When the water wanted something, it rose up
and took it like fathers do mothers.
Like boys do to girls to become men.

We left everything we didn't want on the banks:
once-practiced instruments, laceless shoes,
the feral newborns, blind and starved in a sack.
Committed everything once and for all to silt,
to down-river, to somewhere else entirely.

Kneeling in the reeds, we felt biblical.
Each thing was our own blue-eyed child,
and the reflections on the water's surface
made the branches above us look like out-of-reach crowns.

Like that current, we could get what we wanted by lying down.
We were the most beautiful we'd ever be
emerging from the reeds, dresses consecrated,
every stitch the color of clay.

Jenny Molberg

Marvels of the Invisible

With your new Microset Model I, you will discover marvels of the invisible.

The night I find my father's toy microscope
in the hospital-cold of the empty house,
I dream of him, a boy in 1964. He crosses the yard,
kneels beneath the sprawling live oak,
and fills his specimen jar with fire ants.
His father, in the garage, sings softly in German,
mounting the head of a deer shot
that winter; its antlers blossom like capillaries.
My father is six years old. The light
spills in as he bends over the microscope
and folds a single ant into a plastic slide. The body,
almost sickening in its translucence,
curls into itself; the bright red thorax, close up,
is butterscotch. Pressed beneath the plastic,
the antennae shiver and are still.

Half a century later, my mother's breasts
are removed. In the waiting room, my father
takes a pen from his white coat pocket,
and clicks open, and clicks closed.
When someone in the family asks
a question, he takes a walk. I go with him,
and we wind through orange-tiled hallways.
He shows me the room full of microscopes.
I imagine his eye, how it descends

like a dark blue planet,
and his breath as it clouds the lens.
He shows me the refrigerator
where they keep the malignant tissue.
He shows me the microtomes,
the biopsy needles, the organ baths.

In the recovery room, we listen
as my mother's new systems of blood vessels
shush through a speaker in the room.
My father comes in quietly,
places a white orchid beside her bed.
The large white blossoms are hands
cupping the empty air. Suspended there
is everything that came before this:
the day my parents met,
the wedding, each of the three children
so different from the last. His hands,
that know, like breathing, every inch of her.
He matches his breath with hers,
as they do each night
in the slow river of a breathing house,
and beneath her skin, her blood blossoms.

NOMINATED BY THE UNIVERSITY OF NORTH TEXAS CREATIVE WRITING PROGRAM

Erin Rodoni

Two Nights in Room Nineteen

"She dreamed of having a room or a place, anywhere, where she could go and sit, by herself, no one knowing where she was."
— *Doris Lessing*

Twin queens tucked neat as presents.
The milk in my breasts hardens like evidence.

How many heroines have died of such a room?
But there's no gas noosing its slow lasso, no arsenic

burlesquing feather-light negligees. Only snow
mothed to plate-glass, a breast pump's

hydraulic rasp. When my daughter drinks
she retreats so deep beneath the luminosity

of her skin. I am custodian of every crease
and pore, fine-toothed comb of toes, each nick

named bone. Milk defrosts in a distant kitchen.
She accepts a bottle as evidence. A physicality

to this disconnect, like the gloaming after sex.
Her father softening against my thigh, smooth

and gelatinous as some shy creature
haunting a deep-sea crevasse. I thought of that

when they slapped her brined boneless body
to my chest. The first time I took a boy

in my mouth I didn't know what to do
with all that living gratitude.

Since then my body has learned
how to give thanks, a lesson

it can never forget. Still, I flush
the milk like evidence.

Lenea Grace

Yukon River

We paddle nights,
carve jays in beryl
waters, the salmon luster
cast of a generous latitude,
the forgiving morning.
We have our routines.

You will fry granola
mid-current, rest
the teetery stove
between calves,
browned—

sugar the pan,
enameled with buttery
soap and pinecone
flecks, the filmy
ashes of late

night chats with Germans,
the singing Germans,
those who wave
from rock beds—

Oh girls, see you
tomorrow night, girls,
see you—

under tarps, thunder
heads, the massive,
the stone faces looming
upon grey slumber,
these Klondike graves—

wooden cribs,
muted. In the tent,
I will place a knife
between us to hold
off the dark.

Jacques J. Rancourt
Open Shed

When I took off into the woods behind my house
where the dusk lays down like a wolf, my mother prayed
I would be kept put. Snow had melted into bogs
twice as deep as I was tall and children in our town
were always drowning. Answered prayer: a volunteer,
our town's only barber, found me pinned beneath
the claws of a wire fence. It took hours
to be found. No helicopter could see me through
the cover of oaks. No dog could sniff me out
because I did not smell like the living. When the news
told stories of teenagers who took their own lives,
took them as if they were something to be carried for awhile
and then dropped, I could understand. In the woods
behind my house, the animals were always dying:
the foxes I found crisscrossed against the stone wall;
the moose's rack that reared up from the mulch,
bugs picking skin off its skull. And like the wind that kicks up
the brush, that turns over all the trees' leaves at once,
what began as frightening soon dulled into nothing.

Between my house and the woods, there was a shed.
I had dreams of sleeping in there while outside
the wolves paced. Once I went inside, the ice stiffening
the hinges, and found tools, a workbench.
But up above, a white owl, large as a boy and frozen
to the rafters, stared down at me. And I stared back.

Afterwards, whenever I heard the wolves, it reminded me
I was still afraid to die. A strange comfort,
that chill. When the barber brought me out of the fog
and into my mother's arms, it wasn't her boy he returned.
Snared on the fence, facedown to the ground and watching
the Witch-hazel before me, its unstoppable blossoms,
my mother echoing off the trunks of trees, I kept
to the dirt, not ready—not yet—to get up and return.

S.H. Lohmann
Lullaby

My father grew up in a house with chains in the walls,
protection to bind its body when the earth quaked

its random rage, splitting itself in varying degrees:
most times just a gentle shiver, the earth's plates shrugging

its blades down his country's long spine.
But sometimes it wracked itself ragged, and china hard-rattled

to bits in its case. I could see scars on my father's chin
from tub's slick lip when he was caught in the bath,

he and his sisters all scratched over with these taut white
marks they don't talk about, but don't hide. *Tenías miedo?*

I asked from his neck at bedtime talks, my face pushed up in the crook
of his throat. *Weren't you afraid you might die?*

I could feel his voice better than I could hear it,
the low quake and rumble, his whiskey whisper: *Pipas,*

but we have more time than life.

Annik Adey-Babinski

Wash Bucket

Golden Shovel after Yusef Komunyakaa's "Yellowjackets"

He
showered with a small sick bird. They stood
together under the barn roof, out there,
bathing in
watery tracechains,

man and bird lathered
silly in
velvet froth,

the blue wings just
blue. No one stopped

the water. By
now we all knew a
man like that was best left to his great
acts. Goofy
medicine, we'd learned, worked. A calmness
came over the farm. He
turned off the water and whinnied

at the morning. He was once
a man who slept in bar bathrooms &
felt nothing. Then
we don't know what happened to the

man. The farm was quiet. The whole
field empty. He was somewhere beautiful,

we hoped. He came back blue-black
and started to give good advice. From the sky

we'd fallen into this world and when we fell
we broke. That was why, he said, climbing on
the main beam of the barn, clamping his
hands around the wood, we loved—to try to get back.

Carey Russell

Mackerel

They lie parallel, a textile
of tails and heads, each
inch iridescent like oil

in sunlight. Their eyes,
a frozen phalanx
of the same singular

expression, push
outward watery prisms.
Grey shadows

tigerstripe the scales
into radiant sections,
a lived wallpaper.

How happy they seem
to be together, collected
selfless. They don't care

they're dead, icepacked
in a mold-pocked crate
dripping on Canal Street.

We talk as if death were a line
to be crossed. But look at them.
Tell me where they end.

NOMINATED BY THE *CUMBERLAND RIVER REVIEW*

Andrea Jurjević

For Yugoslavia's More Fortunate Ones

You killed time, and your livers, under viaducts,
vigilantes of underpasses in thick vinegar haze,

puking by the roadside over tin foil, empty bottles,
toilet paper tubes, buttercups, morning glories.

Days welded. Onions sweated in wood crates
at the market. Fish gutted, their scales

thrown back to the sea—that lax bluish rag
between the port and the smokestacks. The burn off.

You watched busses start routes at 5 a.m.,
considered yourselves above the proletariat

that waited somber under fiberglass stops
for the busses' concertina doors to take them,

then watched those soot-crusted vehicles
bend through intestinal streets—past posters

of Yugoslav bands, their multiethnic disco quaver,
past the greenery of dumpsters. You, vigilante

drifters at school parks under the carob trees,
habitually fucking on beds of sun-scorched papers.

And you, stooped by the betting shop—on its walls
the fixed smile of Lady D, yellowed centerfolds,

Sabrina splashing about in her white bandeau bikini.
Remember that Roma boy who, for years, offered

Dobra pička to passersby, his sister—a reasonably priced
premenstrual pussy—the two of them, arms linked,

beautiful together, like two black orchids?

Wayne Johns
Delirium

So as not to send the body into shock
when you stopped, in secret, I knew

you'd started cutting back the dose.
Didn't I feel myself diminishing,

diminished, as I watched for signs?
Evenings, we'd walk through Blackburn Park,

pausing before those two, nearly fused, trees.
They were shape without name until you

called them poplars. It goes without saying,
I never questioned anything you said.

Depending on the day they seemed
to embrace, or brace for impact.

Like everything that hinges
on perspective, we see most what we want

or fear. When you'd catch me studying your face
I'd fake a smile to see you smiling back.

Each morning, facing backwards
on the train ride into work, I'd stare through

Plexiglas at the scroll of pines, then chain link
wound with barbed wire framing construction sites

where tractors went on gouging the red earth.
Then the tunnel. Then intermittent darkness

and my own sad face looking back.
One morning, emerging from the tunnel,

the train stalled. It felt, somehow, familiar—
a group of strangers, suspended

between here and there. Each of us
mumbling and leaning toward the light.

Lisa Wells

Self-Portrait with Manco

after José Clemente Orozco

1. "ÉCHATE LA OTRA"

and another scrawny dog parades
on the Plaza De Armas, archipelagos
of mange gnawed across his ribs

the girl runs her hand the length
of one mutt's spine with tremulous care
and she is the song advancing

from the bullhorn, bungeed to the roof
of the propane delivery truck, suave call
of a viejito repeating
> *bo-ni-ta…bo-ni-ta*

the city wrapped in static
sings to being

> though the pistil is
twisted. Painfully
pinched

bedded in broad magenta petals

the bougainvillea
blushes, labial

        ...beautiful

Let every wound be dashed
to the hand of a woman.

2. "HOMBRE DE FUEGO"

in sepia, in coke-bottle spectacles, Orozco
scales the scaffold one-handed, frail
with rheumatic fever, toward the nude's turned heel.

Nuns flock, in habit, near my bench
to study the murdered worker's grimace
agonized in perseverating light—they carry

their own shade. For every torqued expression
in the vaultings of the nave: a blister
on the nude ascending

into the cupola.
Burned again by the young Columbian
who spent his breath in my ear
all night   *ay guapa…me lastimas*

How easily we flatter, humiliate,
botch the midlife crisis; snubbed by some
prima ballerina, the paintings unimproved.

Orozco knew—too much touch
gluts sensibility, and seduction's just
another stick-up

nice and slow

>   *Come out of your lie*
> *with your lies up*

3. "LA CHATA"

or get wrecked
with Giaconda divina, in the nearest cantina,
one extra white Marlboro plastered to her lip

brazenly flush with collagen—I ache
to pluck the pale finger and drag

so I guess the Mezcal is working.
I'm fresh as a scalded babe!

Everything touches me.
Giaconda's crush on Morrissey
Her baby fat
Her hand

The lithe boys delivering bowls in the Birria kitchen
with its high wall of brightly painted tile,
fey in their neon

nail polish and hairnets
but how do they bear the trays?
Their arms are whips of silk—my god

am I obvious.
Lust does not resent the lie
sweetening on this beauty's tongue,

a prodigious drunk who claims
she's *never missed anyone*
in all her twenty-one years, yet appears

to miss everything. Need, for example,
beating off in the eaves of 9 Esquinas
where the moon knuckles down

through tall palms
and each frond's edge
an immutable blade—

Gabriella R. Tallmadge
Marriage An Animal Language

When we touch it's animals.
We live in dens, snouts and ends
in the dirt. We frog-eared,
we lick the black off plums.

We sweet? We beast? Ancient,
the memory. Call from an outer face.
We talk in leaf—thought, spine, millions.
I am above you, so below. I grow

of you. Antler, knuckle, snake—cell fall
away from cell, show bone, show meat.
Cape of husk and shell. You are my home,
skin beneath my skin. Cicada hum inside

me nesting near ten years.
In our den we animals we sweet.
We eat limes color of money—
hatch and bloom our blood like seeds.

Christine Adams
Accretion: A Study

Offshore, Thresher sharks gather around
the carcass of a young whale. The Coast

Guard tells us that when the wind blows
east we'll be able to smell the rot for miles.

For now, we're out of range, burning a fire
on the beach after my great uncle's funeral.

Everyone's drunk, arguing about where
his ashes should be scattered, and I'm beginning

to worry that I descend from people who hold on
too tightly. Our basement holds too many boxes

of photographs; the backyard mud spits up mouthfuls
of bones in heavy rain—three dogs, two goldfish

won at the state fair; pet rabbits; the baby bird I found
being eaten alive by ants. The pitch of voices rises near

the cooler of Coronas, the West Coast cousins yelling,
he belongs in his orange grove. I ask myself: how will you

ever be any good at loving if you don't learn to let things go?
I practice, dropping trails of pennies on a hot sidewalk.

Soon, I'll be able to give back the harmonica a lover lent,
and one day I'll learn how to ball up my failures and bitterness

into a fistful, and then drop it. For tonight, though, I'll lull myself
to sleep thinking of those sharks, sated and now gentle, having

only enough. Everyone around me is grabbing plastic spoons.
Someone calls for sandwich bags. They're divvying my

uncle up, and I know my family will keep those dust-filled
bags until a future in-law fishes it out of a cluttered drawer,

and not knowing, throws it away. Please don't let this
happen to me, I want to say. Throw me in the ocean

while my body's still warm. Let me float at the surface;
nourish something hungry; sink fathoms down where light

dissolves; provide a ribbed shelter in heavy water.
I want to think that I could give myself up. That

I could say all this to my mother who lay down next
to our still-warm dead dog—who later said to my father

as he held the stiff body, *you can't just leave her out in the cold.*

Richie Hofmann

After

When the sun broke up the thunderheads,
and dissonance was consigned
to its proper place, the world was at once foreign
and known to me. That was shame
leaving the body. I had lived my life
from small relief to small relief, like a boy pulling a thorn
from his foot. Wet and glistening,
twisting toward light, everything seemed
recognizable again: a pheasant lazily dragging
his plume; the cherries dark and shining
on the trellis; moths hovering cotton-like
over an empty bowl; even myself,
where I reclined against an orange wall,
hopeful and indifferent, like an inscription on a door.

Erin J. Mullikin

Leavings That Change the Future

My grandmother's laundry:　　always hanging　　on the line,

　　　　the line strung up　　between two　　bright blue T's:

you could write hundreds of poems　　about laundry

　　　　and never catch the right scent of it,

the tightening of the nose　　where memory

　　　　moves with purpose　　up through the brain.

*

Not a night passes　　　　when I don't feel　　the stiffness in the bath towels,

　　　　when I don't worry a bar of soap　　against the thin gray washcloth,

its frayed edges beautified　by the enormous tigerlily

　　　　forever blossoming at its center.　　The hard water

from the shower　　leaves small white deposits in my hair.

*

And I could have had   to wash the blackberry stains from my hands

or   I could have been using kitchen scissors to cut   out the signatures

   of clouds.

      In the darkness only found at night,   father yelled at us

for not bringing in the wash.   I wanted to give him a sleeping potion

      and would have, if not for the uproar of bullfrogs

hanging around the edges of the pond. They called out for the ways

      in which we know not to put a certain berry in our mouths.

They knew routine and pattern;   they did what they were told by instinct

   what to do,

      just like the sheets that have always made certain shapes when hit by

   the wind,

 a series of wings naming the thing that unfolds inside me.

Corey Miller

Willow Lake Mine

Because I am so fragile
a beard would break me,
it was an easy promise
to keep to never work the mines

like my father,
an easy walk along the strip pits
where I'd pretend the cattails
were the brittle hair

of beauty and not the tender nails
of death. Tender the pink
inside my lungs, tender the snow
inside my voice, tender

the nails of death when my father
found a miner pinned by his own machine
against a wall of coal and expected him to look embarrassed,
but he didn't. He looked like a caryatid supporting nothing,

not even himself, and then they buried him in a suit
instead of his obsidian-kissed coveralls
as though he'd died at a business meeting
or been killed by one,

which he had,
and then they shut the whole mine down
for good, but I was spared all of this
because I am so fragile,

though my father likes to think
I'm strong, likes to tell me
even German can seem pretty
when it's sung.

Daniel Bohnhorst

In Aleppo

A little girl roams through the abandoned bedrooms of her neighbors.

She carries the snub-nosed rifle her father hands her each morning before
she leaves the apartment.

She is searching for a new teddy bear amid the cartridges and broken glass.

At every street crossing, she sprints through alleys of bedsheets the last
civilians have strung up between buildings so the snipers cannot see,
though she is just a little girl, why should they fire.

To the bloodshot eye at the viewfinder, she is a borderless ripple of air behind
the linen, an enemy no more definite than joy itself.

In her nightmare, the snipers encircle her—one bullet shatters her
breastbone, another divides her shoulder blades—but waking, she takes
up her rifle and continues the hunt.

In her growing skull, in her lungs expanding still, in the small bones of her
ribcage spreading a little wider each hour, with a tattered bear under her
arm, she defies the nightly news.

Tilling the streets in her odyssey, she prepares the ancient city for the day
when its birds will return.

Anders Carlson-Wee
Icefisher

The man sets the fish house far out
on the lake. Drills the hole.
Scoops the slush out with a ladle.
Silence and the lake and the man.
The pine hills folded in fog,
faded to ash and gun powder.
The maple leaves fallen and lost
in the snow. The gray ghost
thin and sinewy, moving off through
the coal-black remnants of branches.
If you cannot see it in winter
you will never see it.
The man goes into the dark house
and lowers his lure. The deep hole
glows. The water is clear.
The low hoot of the owl simmers
the shore meridian as the evening
comes on and the hole
darkens. He breathes into his hands.
He lets out a little more line.

Benjamin Goldberg
The Gospel According to Rust

Brother, didn't I build us a solace
in the jaws of junkyard Dobermans:

tarpaulin roofs over rusted Caddy
chassises, PVC pipe rafters elbow-

jointed and chained to a graveyard
of empty propane tanks? You called

the whole mess of survival *too city
for us to live in*. You called falling

in love with anything that couldn't
give you tetanus being *hex-screwed*

or *hobnailed*. Off-grid, our country
bounded by chain link, you coaxed

any hour we needed from the hands
of broken clocks. I called you *pyro-*

mancer, rubble-rouser. Childhoods
burned into and sprang from less ash

than we used to fill our mason jars.
When we moved to an iron trellis,

you prepared by slaughtering a library.
You stuffed pizza box mattresses

with pages ripped from the world
you vowed to unwrite. You gagged

the leather-bound mouth of a bible
with nails my body had reddened.

You saved these for the palms
of any man who tried to save us.

Christopher Citro

Gathering a Few Facts

It's enough on this Monday morning that I can
remember the difference between a thorn
and a prickle and it appears as if I'll actually be
getting to work on time. It's the same time
as it always is in this parking garage,
sodium lamp time, who's walking suspiciously
behind the car time, what would I do if
someone put a gun in through my window time.
Can a travel mug of hot tea work as a
weapon of self defense? I know I wouldn't
want any poured on me, but then again
I'm not a criminal. I'm soft. A true thorn
is a modified branch and a prickle is something
to do with the skin only. Most roses have
prickles not thorns, which is disappointing
on so many levels and the kind of thing I have
to carry around with me as well as manage
morning traffic. I'm keeping it together.
I'm not harassing other people in their cars.
I see us, many of us, sitting behind the wheel
for a moment or two, gathering one or two
firm facts to ourselves before gritting our teeth
and stepping onto the streets where nobody loves us.

Nicole Rollender

Gettysburg

When he found the calf
bone in the endless cornfield past

the quiet barn—filled with old, dust-
covered clocks, sturdy dark Morris chair frames, bird

spines, their tiny skulls, the architecture of wings—
your grandfather was unfazed. A lopsided bullet caught

in yellow bone. He said, *I've found another one,*
and added it to the bag out in the shed.

The first time we came here together, field stretching
far back to mountain, was a beginning of slow

knowledge of the body, its ancient rhymes and drifts
into grace. We rode thick horses across the battlefield

at twilight, green as soul light rising above peat bogs.
The dead don't speak. Yet, across the world young Windeby Girl

curls in bog mud, arranged by kind hands after hanging
for adultery. Thin curved twigs woven through her ribs as a death

wreath and, oh, what remains of her hair survives through centuries,
a bright star rising in the mud. Death is everywhere.

In a Roman grave, two unearthed skeletons hold hands, finger bones
crossed over pelvises, bracelets still on wrists. And here, behind

the barn, your great-grandmother found a soldier's belt buckle,
his whole skeleton buried near an oak tree, his buttons and spoons

intact. The dead don't speak. You don't have to believe that. Here
as darkness descends into fog between trees, doors are opening out

of this world. Single bones gleam alone between rocks. Maybe what
the dead want is for you to speak their names for the last time—

after that, they can die untethered from the earth forever. Someone
lingers between goldenrod and fence, holding his broad hand out

to a lamb, its mouth opening to what strange, delicious flower he offers.

Rosanna Oh

Erasures

For my father

In our house, none of the pencils have erasers.
That's a sign of dutiful children, my father jokes
and, therefore, successful parents.

How long it has been since he's written,
I do not know. But today, my father
and his friends have taken leave

of their groceries and liquor stores
to visit the local Buddhist temple
for a famous monk's sermon on the nature of greed,

which my father raised me to believe
is a virtue. A pencil rests on the thorax
of my father's thumb, callused

from lifting boxes of produce
and sharpening knives. The monk draws
a circle on the chalkboard and asks in Korean,

"Must greed exist in the service of others?"
A man dressed up in a suit, sitting
in the front row, says, "Yes." It's his second

correct answer. My father bows his head, rubs
the eraser on the paper, then writes
the other man's answer.

My father's page has become as gray
as the chalkboard, which is covered
in circles and Korean words

I wish I could understand.
My old man takes his time with writing
his notes, as though he's trying to remember

what it means to cut out words and to write
them down, to select his memories
for future reference. At one moment,

he writes quickly while nodding his head;
at the next, he leans over to my mother
so she can repeat a phrase the monk has just said.

I wonder whether my father's always lived
this carefully, as though in fear of regret,
even before he immigrated to the U.S.

Maybe he's erased too much of himself
in his pursuit of a "life" in the word's
most conventional sense:

sacrifice, money, shelter, family.
On the other hand, isn't that what survival is—
to forget a dead parent, to say goodbye

to one's country, to dismiss one's greed
for things that couldn't be?
My father's too embarrassed to share

his dreams with me, though my mother
once revealed that he was a writer
in his youth until I was born. She said

his favorite story is the myth of Odysseus.
Neither she nor I know the reason
for the attraction. I suppose it might be

the prospect of uncertainty the waters offer
while the hero, circling and circling
the desolate isles, lives at the mercy of a god.

Or maybe it's the taboo allure of the island women,
or the luxury of fooling them
into thinking his body,

even after a decade of fighting,
is still as whole as it was in Ithaca.
The travails of one man can feed

the imagination of another.
I'd like to believe my father has chosen
to remember Odysseus's homecoming.

In that part of the story, moving on
is judged a necessity, as is confronting
the unwritten struggles awaiting the hero.

My father's page is almost full.
He blows eraser dust off his page.
He repeats to himself:

"Greed must exist in the service of others."
People say I am my father's daughter—
Perhaps the remark

is intended as a prophecy.
I erase the circles I've doodled on my page.
I start to write.

Quinn Lewis

Flora and Fauna: Eyarth Station, Ruthin, North Wales

for my uncle

There in the summered north country,
where gusty breeze and wild violets bloomed
in scattered beds about the roadside,
where the railway station had turned
white-washed hotel, where Tara, dusty
golden brown, unbridled, grazed
just beyond the wooden fence of our hotel,
and everything
was that green-gold hint of light
in childhood: there I see us standing,
the sign for Llanfair hidden
behind hedgerows and the wings
of common blues and small heath
butterflies too delicate to land,
everything more brilliant than before.
You, as tall as southern cypress,
and I, a broom shrub, held sugar cubes
in the palms of our hands
for Tara, who would not come,
keeping our thumbs pressed flat
against the other fingers.
How I begged, when finally she did
approach, for you to lift me up
past the fence rails and into the dip
of her bare back where I would have fit

so nicely. No, the hoteliers wouldn't like it.
How I cried, my little, narrow voice
never reaching past the hills of limestone,
but reaching you. In daydreams
(tonight I will dream my father dying,
not you, and I, and all, will be inconsolable),
sometimes in daydreams, I see
your cypresses swaying dark green
under gray light in the near rain
of an Alabama, April afternoon.
I see your seven dogs escape
to the back porch of the house you built
in Ruthin's image, downpour flooding
the gravel drive, the rosebush beds,
the walled garden you made and left
unfinished in the side yard.
Who will tend it now? Who will stand
in your kitchen and scatter salt
from tiny spoons over egg yolks
like half-moons? Let's talk
of cypresses. I'll let you lead me
around the grounds of your house,
like you used to. I won't complain.
Then let us go, once more walking down,
down the sooty road in Ruthin—
Tara, Tara—talk of asphodel, herb Robert, little
tormentil, hound's tongue, light blue
harebell. Let's listen—meadow pipit rustling
in the purple saxifrage of morning, or the first

eyebrights of the season.
Your ashes will be buried.
There, the raven. There,
the scattered grains of limestone.
I wish I knew what mattered:
that we were there,
that we are not there anymore.

Brittney Scott
The Money Shot

I'll shave everything in advance,
beginning with the delicate bend behind the knee
that feels like a sexual artery,
a tendon that could be cut
without much effort,
a pale patch that burns
after the first close shearing.

Next, the always loose older elbow,
so dry and unlady-like.
Every safety is sacrificed.
The way I must prop my leg up and bow
to reach with my three-bladed razor,
the pieces of myself I must pull over.

More animal than doll, like an ostrich
down in the dirt, a porcupine,
a loose-necked hen with her wattle
swinging about.
And then, I guess I should kneel
and let you own it.

I'll open my mouth, bare my begging uvula
so my guts coat with saliva, which they do
naturally when I'm going to vomit.
This is the acme, the moment

when all the men grab harder and push,
stretch their thick-veined necks
back and moan,
exposing their throbbing throats.

Iliana Rocha

Looking at Women

My father taught me how. His curious eyes, perpetually amber from
drinking, would scan a woman, rest on a bold curve they liked: tits or
ass. He was not a leg man. It would begin innocently enough, his arm
draped across a bench at the mall, my mother shopping. I'd sit in his
armpit, matted hair in Old Spice, while his gaze trucked each body
teetering on stilettos. Weekends, my father watched *Sábado Gigante*.
Would hoot & holler at the women wearing nothing but dark
eyebrows & overdrawn lips, occasionally an accordion as a dress.
¡Damn! he would exclaim. Damn. There were also the pornos, soft-
core, half-naked women with their hard breasts mistakenly attached to
ribs. "Hot blonde" was a universal phrase, & brunettes became sexy
only when they removed their glasses & shook their tight buns loose
from their heads. Teachers can be hot too. Sometimes I slept on the
living room sofa, & the TV's glare would wake me: nude mermaids
fingering each other in the gills, merman sucking their shiny pennies
of nipple. Then there was the internet history. More women—some
pregnant, some just chubby. I noticed my own body, legs half-tree
trunk, half-lightning rod. Tried to pinch the skin around my knees &
ankles into neater shapes. A waist strangled into a waist: el número
ocho, la guitarra. Some have found that waist, others reached right
through it to other women everywhere: one positioned obediently in
the emptiness of one boyfriend's computer screen, sunny & grinning
in bikini. Continuous others popped up, contained in rectangles,
snapping a thong's hot pink. I started to look, too, at one in a

commercial licking barbecue sauce from her fingers. My stare isn't all that different than his—start from the face, scroll down. I love a woman in a tight dress, made up like a drag queen.

NOMINATED BY THE WESTERN MICHIGAN UNIVERSITY CREATIVE WRITING PROGRAM

Jen Jabaily-Blackburn

For Gene Kelly

Astaire never rang the right
bells in me no sir   I am Gene Kelly's girl always wanted to be
Cyd Charisse rippling off your arm like a sail everywhere
disappearing   reappearing   sometimes it seemed you were pure
energy compressed & desperate to burst   the ballet with Caron in Paris
fucking hell it makes me want to take off all my clothes & then
get more clothes on just to remove them
how did we let you fall out of fashion
it's nothing short of criminal oh you
jester you
            kestrel you
                        lynx you lion   don't look at me I can't explain it
muscles are having a zeitgeist moment
no love left for spark & smolder we like our beefcakes
ostentatious all these abs these delts these
pecs as hard as de-glutenized loaves   Our century's tastes are
questionable   you had muscles but *used* them   our stars are
Range Rovers bought for conquering Brooklyn   it's still
searing to think of your boundless legs failing but I saw it
they trotted you out after the stroke to collect a medal   it was endless
ugly   unholy   an act of
vandalism in a cathedral
            why are they doing this I remember thinking
Xanadu was a mercy next to this
you were going out the way you wanted   the whole giddy future
zooming up on rollerskates   like anything could catch you on rollerskates

Matt Sumper

American Manhood

After Robert Wrigley

Father, what have I learned from you
and not ruined? Bearing down
on your Craftsman chainsaw,
felling trees after grandmother died,
I admired how the heart can level anything.
Watching you vacuum dirt from
her car's back seat, my only thought was
the cost of love. I remember my bedroom
shaking like a damaged submarine
as you slugged the heavy bag
screwed into the basement ceiling,
a steady 1-2 1-2 1-2-3,
a chant of *Mother, mother, where are you?*
Father, did you know I absorbed
those thick concussions,
made them my own? A year later,
I put on a helmet and shoulder pads,
tackled head-first, and smiled
as opponent's bodies seemed to vanish.
When I quit bussing tables,
I punctured each door
of my boss's black sedan
with a salad fork, imagining the doors
were lungs. Father, it's shameful
to admit I feared your grief.

Man of so many quiet years,
you never meant to teach me
these lessons, so they're the ones
I've kept: when you hit
something hard enough, it feels
like nothing, after enough years
in the cold, all rivers turn to ice.

Jeremy Windham

After the Funeral

When the men of my family left to bury my grandfather's sister,
I went home with the women and built a tipi inside myself.

I could have helped heave mounds of wet earth over her casket
and level the loose dirt above her with the backside of a shovel.

I could have driven home with the men in silence instead of tending
my hideaway's hearth and chanting prayers of courage over its flames.

I helped my grandmother unfold checkered linen over the card table
where we sipped microwaved coffee and waited by the telephone.

It was my cousin who answered my father's call two hours later;
the men had finished early, the rain made the dirt easier to move.

By that time I had already leaned imaginary saplings together,
stretched the sun-dried hide of my boyhood over whittled limbs

and crawled inside to flee from the weeping, to remember her alone.
I glanced out the window whose sill she helped paint, failing at first

to recognize her in the fig falling from the tree in our front yard,
the tree that had wilted once before bearing its first round of fruit.

She greeted me as she never had before, called me out from myself
by a snapped stem, a fig split open on the asphalt, wavering, then still.

Lisa Kwong

An AppalAsian Finds Home in Bloomington, Indiana

I call myself an AppalAsian,
an Asian from Appalachia.

I rock leopard print and black stilettos,
write protest emails to Victoria's Secret,
wear Brooks and flat-foot-proof orthotics.

After 5K brunch is a French Tickler,
a ham and cream cheese crepe,
mimosa with cherry. I victory-
dance in the basement stairwell
of Ballantine, break into song
upon hearing the word "lonely."

I travel to Greece and Taiwan
vicariously through the men
I liked. I am from letting go
of the man who left for Florida.

I push up and bird dog,
lemon squeeze and tricep dip
as sweat hisses, every breath
a billowing kite lifting my body
higher and sorer.

I keep a flashlight
in the bathroom, just in case
I have to hunker down
in the bathtub
while a tornado blasts
through the parking lot.

I am from tea parties
and Scrabble, Pink Moscato
and Poeteers, exploding tacos,
chicken and dumplings.

I AppalAsian up this Midwest
college town, eat chicken feet,
mac-n-cheese, celebrate butts
and ancestors. I am from
a fridge covered in babies,
none of them mine,
postcards and handwritten poems
received via snail mail.

I ponder the mirror,
study the woman before me,
see the tear-stained tub of lard,
see the runner's legs,
see the glittering, Cinderella
blue earring heart.

Danielle Jones-Pruett

American Bittersweet

The field near our house didn't want to be a field, it wanted
to grow wild: scrub pines, bittersweet blooms, fuzzy wisps
of arbor vitae. When mama was in the mood for *cleansweeping*,
she'd pull her hair back, put on thick denim overalls, work gloves,
and boots that belonged to a man whose feet I couldn't remember.
She said she liked to spend Sunday on her knees, and she'd pull
up a shrub, roots running down her arms like muddy veins,
like Jesus's heart on the outside of his body. Sometimes
she'd rock on her heels, and I'd know not to ask for lunch or supper.
You see, when you look out your car window, you think *that's always been,
will always be, a field*. But that's not the truth: all fields want
to grow up. When mama looks out the kitchen window, all she sees
is the field where her oldest daughter was last seen running,
and she'll *be goddamned* if she's going to let that field
turn back to forest.

Chuck Carlise

I Can Tell You a Story

It's the middle of night, & I've rolled toward Katie,
kissed her shoulder—
    something I do in these hours, she says,
  though I never remember.
She puts two fingertips on my temple,
brushes hair behind my ear,
 as I float on the cloud-edge of waking.

I think these are her favorite moments—
    the helpless honesty of half-sleep,
where there are no words to parse or doubt,
  & a kiss can only mean
      I'm glad you're here.

Listen—I can tell you a story, but not all of it:

  I can tell you blue ink, how the nights ran together,
  how I'd wake to her breathing, ashen & full;
 I can tell you the window she never kept closed,
      the shadows of trees
 & her voice—a whisper, *okay, okay.*

Listen—there is no way to end this.
No matter how it begins, how many times.

On a cliffside, over another city,
      clouds sprawl like a quilt.
Beneath them: thick drizzle,
   grey darkness. Above,
  red-orange dusk. A dream of music.

What if we change the names? What if apologies?
       If the pilot light's out?
  What if we're on a boardwalk, in the summer,
      the whole world flashing & deep-fried?
If the song were about someone else, on a highway,
    a broken promise & so many ways to regret?
An idea of home left in a bus seat? In a notebook?
      In a payphone in Sicily, at dawn, the words so distant
she heard them on a whole different day?

What if all this was gone? If a decade could pass? Our fears
    grow hearts of their own? What if the grand gesture
  is too small? If we've failed each other
        one time too far?

What would it take to wake again to that darkness,
                    that hesitance & shudder?
Such delicate breath.

God, how do we ever forgive ourselves?

Karen Malzone

Quiet Moon and Harvested Fields

I want to find my father's body tonight
in the river, face-up,
hands flurrying weeds below,
drifting with currents.

It's been years since river
saturated his swim trunks
as he swam, chasing muskrats
with boyhood sweetness. I want

his tired skin to feel algae's soft jubilance
clinging to leg hairs, making his whole being
part river, part turtle and scale
as shad nose his calves past recognition,
imagining he is one of their school.

Some nights, this river swallows stars,
its blood grows constellate, lit
from the bottom by all its moons;
they bow and sing.

But now I want him
cupped in these black heavens,
carried downstream, singing lower
and louder than the moon.

I think of what the water remembers,
hemmed by bulrushes and reeds.

All the river silvers, even that
held in my father's navel, that
which fills his ears, and carves red clay-
rooted shores deeper and broader.

Come in. There is a low tide tonight, the water
crisp and celestial-shallow. My father's body,
luminous and safe, beacons in the current,
calls to the heron, the harbor, my feet in soft mud at the bank.

NOMINATED BY THE DREW UNIVERSITY MFA PROGRAM
IN POETRY AND POETRY IN TRANSLATION

Karen Embry

My Love Affair with Darth Vader

It started sometime in late fall, early winter. When feeling became
unnecessary. A point of protection. He had red skin underneath it all
and I thought it might be something not unlike kindness. Him: all the
time coming on to me with heavy breathing and constant surprises under
that big black cape. Me: hiding in trash cans because I did not want to
bother him. I pretended to be looking for loose change when he found
me fumbling through papers, smelling of old fruit and yesterday's meat.
He took me for walks. We watched the sunset together. He promised me
the Empire. I baked him cupcakes and a rump roast, which he ate while
giving orders to an army of men. I hid R2-D2 from him, but eventually
I had to turn the poor guy in. Brought him to his chambers with ribbons
in exchange for a gloved hand and slow deep breaths. I tried to explain my
story. I wanted to make him happy. He said I wasn't funny. Shortly after
that he became bored. Stopped playing nice. Started blowing things up.
That's when I figured out he was my father. Always like a clown in that big
black mask. Always pretending to be someone he was not.

T.J. Sandella
Kayaking, Early Morning

Surely, if god exists
he'll choose now to speak with me.
Now being the perfect time,
considering just ahead on the river
there is the crane's cadence—
how it weaves in and out of the sunlight
piercing the trees, how the oak's leaves
drift from their branches
to settle on water, sending ripples
into orbit—an echo to fall's arrival.

But I'm too easily distracted
by beauty. Con men can smell me—
sell me anything if it's shiny
and symmetrical.

Even these solitary trips
downriver leave me vulnerable.
And if god appeared
to talk to me, man to man,
hombre a hombre,
forfeiting his guises of burning bushes
and thunder and lightning,
I'd probably forget myself
and firmly shake his hand—even thank him,
perhaps, for the birds,
all that business with the sun.

I wouldn't ask
about war, famine, or natural disasters
and I certainly wouldn't inquire
about Mom's recurring cancer
or blue-faced overdosed sisters.

With so much sleight-of-hand splendor,
he could come and he could go,
and no one could ever say he didn't give
at least one of us a chance to understand
this misery, this bewildering beauty.

Amanda Jane McConnon
Life on Earth

If you go out too far from this earth
the heat from your body becomes enough

to boil water. No need to tempt ourselves
to revolt against us in that way.

See, that far out the world is smooth
and manageable, its highest mountains

unsubstantial as dust on a cue ball.
And if you feel like being grateful,

know that the largest meteor
ever destined for you was so flat

it skipped across the atmosphere
like a stone, which it was. So while many

tragedies have made it to you,
countless more have lost

their course along the way.
And if that isn't enough, know

there is a tiny amount of gold in each scoop
of seawater, that each drop, at some point,

has passed over something shining and held it.
If you try, you can get so quiet you become

your own planet, and then it's natural,
even necessary that some parts

of you stay dark while others
spend their measured time in the light.

Contributors' Notes

CHRISTINE ADAMS is a recent graduate of the University of North Carolina at Greensboro MFA Program. During her time in North Carolina, she was awarded the Fred Chappell Fellowship, and served as poetry editor for the *Greensboro Review*. She is the recipient of two Academy of American Poets Prizes, and was the first runner-up in the 2012 *Ploughshares* Emerging Writer's Contest. She lives and works in Washington, DC.

ANNIK ADEY-BABINSKI is a Canadian studying for her MFA in poetry at Florida International University, where she is a John S. and James L. Knight Fellow. She has recently had poems and translations published in *Salamander*, *Hobart*, and *Jai-Alai* magazines.

NICO ALVARADO teaches middle school in Colorado.

KATE ANGUS is a founding editor of Augury Books and the creative writing advisor for The Mayapple Center for Arts and Humanities. Her work has appeared in *Indiana Review, Subtropics, Court Green, Verse Daily,* the *Awl,* the *Hairpin,* the *Toast,* and *Best New Poets 2010*. She is the recipient of an A Room of Her Own Foundation "Orlando" Prize, the *Southeastern Review*'s Narrative Nonfiction prize and a Wildfjords artists residency in Westfjords, Iceland.

MIRIAM BIRD GREENBERG is the author of two chapbooks: *All night in the new country* (Sixteen Rivers Press) and *Pact-Blood, Fever Grass* (Ricochet Editions).

She's held fellowships from the Provincetown Fine Arts Work Center, the Poetry Foundation, and the National Endowment for the Arts, and was a Wallace Stegner Fellow in Poetry at Stanford University. She lives in Berkeley and teaches ESL, though she's also crossed the continent by bicycle and freight train, deckhanded aboard sailboats, and hitchhiked on four continents.

LINDA BLASKEY is the recipient of two fellowship grants from Delaware Division of Art. Her chapbook, *Farm*, won the Dogfish Head Poetry Prize and the Delaware Press Association's Communications Contest. She is poetry editor for the *Broadkill Review*. She grew up in the Ozark Mountains of Arkansas and now lives in the flat lands of southern Delaware.

DANIEL BOHNHORST was born and raised in Minneapolis. His poems have recently appeared or are forthcoming in various recycling centers across Northern New Mexico. He has received fellowship from many people. He lives in Santa Fe, where he works in violin repair.

CHUCK CARLISE was born in Canton, Ohio, on the first Flag Day of the Jimmy Carter Administration, and has lived in a dozen states and two continents since. He is the author of the chapbooks *A Broken Escalator Still Isn't the Stairs* (Concrete Wolf, 2011) and *Casual Insomniac* (Bateau, 2011), and the recipient of the Inprint Paul Verlaine Poetry Prize, two Dorothy Sargent Rosenberg Prizes, and the C.T. Wright/Academy of American Poets Prize. He studied at Wittenberg University and UC-Davis before completing his PhD at the University of Houston, where he served as nonfiction editor of the journal *Gulf Coast*. His poems and essays can be found in the *Southern Review, Pleiades, Hayden's Ferry Review*, and elsewhere. He can be found at www.chuckcarlise.com.

ANDERS CARLSON-WEE was a professional rollerblader before he studied wilderness survival and started hopping freight trains to see the country.

He is the winner of *Ninth Letter*'s 2014 Poetry Award, *New Delta Review*'s 2014 Editors' Choice Prize, and a Dorothy Sargent Rosenberg Poetry Prize. His work has appeared or is forthcoming in *Blackbird, Ninth Letter, Grist, Linebreak*, the *Paris-American, Best New Poets 2012*, and elsewhere. A recipient of scholarships from the Bread Loaf Writers' Conference and the Sewanee Writers' Conference, Anders is currently an MFA candidate in poetry at Vanderbilt University.

CHRISTOPHER CITRO's first book of poetry, *The Maintenance of the Shimmy-Shammy*, is forthcoming from Steel Toe Books in 2015. His recent and upcoming publications include poetry in *Prairie Schooner, Ninth Letter, Subtropics, Third Coast, Salamander*, the *Pinch*, the *Hollins Critic*, and *Verse Daily*, and creative nonfiction in *Colorado Review*. He received his MFA in poetry from Indiana University and lives in Syracuse, New York.

NOEL CROOK's book, *Salt Moon*, was chosen for the 2013 *Crab Orchard Review* First Book Award and is forthcoming from Southern Illinois University Press. Her poems have appeared in *River Styx, Shenandoah, Smartish Pace*, and other journals. She holds an MFA in creative writing at North Carolina State University and is currently a poetry editor for S_U_N_ Books & Editions.

KAREN EMBRY received her MA in English/creative writing from California State University, Sacramento and her PhD in English from the University of California, Davis. Her poems have appeared in *Poetry Now*, the *Santa Clara Review*, the *Suisun Valley Review*, the *Pomona Valley Review*, and *Calaveras Station*.

SARA GELSTON is the recipient of fellowships and awards from the Wisconsin Institute for Creative Writing, The Fine Arts Work Center in Provincetown, and the University of Illinois, where she received her MFA. Her recent work appears in *Ploughshares, Poetry Northwest, Versal, Big Big Wednesday*,

Verse Daily, Third Coast, and other places. Originally from Maine, she lives with her partner, poet Max Somers, in the Midwest.

BENJAMIN GOLDBERG's poems have appeared or are forthcoming in *TriQuarterly, Ninth Letter, Hayden's Ferry Review*, the *Greensboro Review, Devil's Lake, Salt Hill*, and elsewhere. He is the recipient of an award from The Bread Loaf Writers' Conference, and was a finalist for the 2014 *Vinyl 45* Chapbook Contest, the 2013 *Third Coast* Poetry Prize, the 2013 *New Millennium Writings* Award for Poetry, and the 2012 *Southeast Review* Gearhart Poetry Contest. He lives with his wife outside Washington, DC, and began his MFA at Johns Hopkins University this fall. Find him online at www.benrgold.com.

LENEA GRACE is a Canadian writer whose work has appeared in *Washington Square, Contemporary Verse 2, Riddle Fence*, and online at the *Best American Poetry* site. A graduate of the MFA program at The New School, Lenea is the founding editor of the *Mackinac*, an online poetry magazine. She lives in Toronto.

RICHIE HOFMANN is the recipient of a Ruth Lilly Poetry Fellowship, and his poems have appeared or are forthcoming in the *New Yorker, Ploughshares, Kenyon Review*, and *Poetry*. He is currently a creative writing fellow in poetry at Emory University. His debut collection of poems, *Second Empire*, winner of the Beatrice Hawley Award, is forthcoming from Alice James Books in November 2015.

JEN JABAILY-BLACKBURN lives in Northampton, Massachusetts, where she works as an administrative assistant with the Poetry Center at Smith College. She holds an MFA from the University of Arkansas. Other poems have appeared or are scheduled to appear in *Sycamore Review, Subtropics,*

Unsplendid, cream city review, Hayden's Ferry Review, and the *Journal*, among other publications.

WAYNE JOHNS has published work in *New England Review, Ploughshares, Prairie Schooner, Image, court green*, and elsewhere. His poetry manuscript *Words Without Songs* has been a finalist for the Wick Poetry Prize and the National Poetry Series, among others. His first published fiction was a short story selected by Scott Heim as runner-up for the 2013 *BLOOM* Fiction Chapbook Prize. He has been a recent resident at the Vermont Studio Center and a 2014 Lambda Writers Retreat Fellow in fiction. He's currently working on a novel (tentatively titled *Where Your Children Are*) set in his hometown of Atlanta, Georgia.

DANIELLE JONES-PRUETT holds an MFA from the University of Massachusetts Boston and is program coordinator for the Writers House at Merrimack College. Her work has appeared or is forthcoming in *Bateau, Beloit Poetry Journal, Southern Poetry Review*, and others. Danielle is a recipient of a 2014 Rona Jaffe Foundation Writer's Award.

ANDREA JURJEVIĆ's poems have recently appeared or are forthcoming in the *Journal, Harpur Palate, Raleigh Review, Midwest Quarterly*, the *Missouri Review*, and elsewhere. She is the 2013 Robinson Jeffers Tor Prize Winner. A native of Croatia, she lives in Atlanta, Georgia, where she writes, translates and teaches English.

LISA KWONG earned her MFA in poetry at Indiana University Bloomington. A native of Virginia, she is a two-time Frost Place scholarship recipient, a Neal-Marshall Graduate Fellow, and the winner of the Guy Lemmon Award in Public Writing and the inaugural Asian Pacific American Inspiration Award at Indiana University. Her poems are forthcoming or have appeared in *Naugatuck River Review, Banango Street, Appalachian Heritage, pluck! The Affrilachian Journal of Arts & Culture*, and other journals. She currently teaches at Indiana University and coordinates the Fountain Square Poetry Series in Bloomington, Indiana.

PETER LABERGE is an undergraduate student at the University of Pennsylvania. His poetry appears in *PANK,* the *Louisville Review, Weave Magazine, DIAGRAM*, and *Hanging Loose*, among others. He currently co-edits *Poets on Growth* (Math Paper Press, 2015), and serves as the founder and editor-in-chief of the *Adroit Journal.* His debut chapbook, *Hook*, is forthcoming from Sibling Rivalry Press.

QUINN LEWIS is currently pursuing her MFA in poetry at the University of Oregon. Her work has appeared in *Birmingham Poetry Review.*

S.H. LOHMANN has her MFA from Hollins University, where she was a graduate assistant and assistant editor of the *Hollins Critic.* Her work has been honored with the 2012 Melanie Hook Rice Award in Narrative Nonfiction, the 2011 Gertrude Claytor Poetry Prize from the Academy of American Poets, and a 2010 artist grant from the Baltimore Office of Promotion and the Arts. Her poetry has appeared in the *Indiana Review, Rattle*, and *Third Coast.* She lives in Roanoke, Virginia, where she runs programming for English literacy education to adult immigrants and refugees at Blue Ridge Literacy. She is from Texas.

KAREN MALZONE teaches poetry and creative writing to high school students in Central New Jersey. The rest of her time is spent puttering about the Delaware River, traveling, and creating an awe-filled racket. She holds an MFA in poetry from Drew University.

AMANDA JANE MCCONNON is from an almost-shore town in New Jersey. She has an MFA from New York University. Her poetry has previously appeared in *BOXCAR Poetry Review, Columbia: A Journal of Literature and Art*, and others.

COREY MILLER holds an MFA from the Michener Center for Writers and will be the Philip Roth resident at Bucknell for fall 2014. Recent work can be found in *Narrative* and *Forklift, Ohio*.

MATTHEW MINICUCCI's first full-length collection, *Translation*, was chosen by Jane Hirshfield for the 2014 Wick Poetry Prize and will be published by Kent State University Press in 2015. His work has also appeared in or is forthcoming from numerous journals including the *Cincinnati Review*, the *Gettysburg Review*, the *Massachusetts Review*, the *Southern Review*, and *West Branch*, among others. He currently teaches writing at the University of Illinois at Urbana–Champaign.

JENNY MOLBERG is the 2014 winner of the Berkshire Prize and her debut collection of poems, *Marvels of the Invisible*, is forthcoming from Tupelo Press in 2016. Her work has appeared in *North American Review*, the *New Guard*, *Copper Nickel, Mississippi Review, Third Coast, Smartish Pace, Louisville Review* and elsewhere. Currently, she is the production editor of *American Literary Review* and a doctoral candidate at the University of North Texas.

RACHEL MORGENSTERN-CLARREN is a poet and Portuguese-English translator, as well as the Dispatches editor for *Words Without Borders*. Her work has been honored with a Fulbright Fellowship, a Hopwood Award, an Academy of American Poets Prize, and an artist's grant from the Vermont Studio Center. She was a 2013 Ruth Lilly Fellowship finalist. Her poems appear or are forthcoming in journals including *Narrative*, the *Common*, *Michigan Quarterly Review*, *Passages North*, and *Painted Bride Quarterly*. She holds an MFA in poetry and literary translation from Columbia University.

ERIN J. MULLIKIN is the author of the chapbook *Strategies for the Bromidic* (dancing girl press), and her poems, short fiction, and book reviews have appeared or are forthcoming in magazines such as *elsewhere, Coldfront, ILK, Tammy, Spork, alice blue review*, and *Birdfeast*. She is the former editor-in-chief for *Salt Hill Journal* and a founding editor for *NightBlock* and Midnight City Books. She teaches at Syracuse University.

C.L. O'DELL was born in Suffern, New York, and received his MFA in poetry at Manhattanville College. His poems are published in *Ploughshares, New England Review, Barrow Street, Southern Indiana Review* and *Blackbird*, among others. He is founder and editor of the *Paris-American*, a poetry e-zine and reading series at Poets House in New York City.

ROSANNA OH holds degrees from the University of Wisconsin-Madison, the Writing Seminars at Johns Hopkins University, and Yale University. Her writing has appeared or is forthcoming in the *Common, Measure, cellpoems*, and other publications. She also has been nominated for the Pushcart Prize and Best of the Net, and is one of the inaugural winners of the "Poetry Unites—My Favorite Poem" contest hosted by the Academy of American Poets. She lives in Jericho, New York.

JOY PRIEST is a writer living in the In-Between where she was born and raised. She has been accepted to *Callaloo Journal* and Bread Loaf's creative writing workshops, and at 25 she is one of the newest and youngest members of the Affrilachian Poets. Joy is the recipient of an Emerging Artist Award from the Kentucky Arts Council and her work can be found in *pluck! The Affrilachian Journal of Arts & Culture, Still: The Journal, Toe Good Poetry Journal, Solstice Literary Magazine,* and on her website at joypriest.com.

JACQUES J. RANCOURT was raised in Maine. His poems have appeared or will appear in *Kenyon Review, Virginia Quarterly Review,* and *New England Review,* among others. A former Stegner Fellow, he lives in Oakland, California.

ILIANA ROCHA is originally from Texas and is currently a PhD candidate in English/creative writing at Western Michigan University. She earned her MFA in creative writing/poetry from Arizona State University, where she was poetry editor for *Hayden's Ferry Review.* Her work has previously appeared or is forthcoming in *Blackbird, Yalobusha Review, Puerto del Sol,* and *Third Coast.* Her first book, *Karankawa,* won the 2014 AWP Donald Hall Prize in Poetry and will be published by the University of Pittsburgh Press.

ERIN RODONI earned her MFA in poetry from San Diego State University. Her poems have appeared or will appear in *Colorado Review, Verse Daily, Tupelo Quarterly, Chautauqua, Cumberland River Review,* and others. She won a 2013 Intro Journals Award from AWP. She lives in the San Francisco Bay Area with her husband and two-year-old daughter.

NICOLE ROLLENDER is the author of the poetry chapbooks *Absence of Stars* (forthcoming July 2015, dancing girl press & studio), *Little Deaths* (forthcoming November 2015, ELJ Publications), and *Arrangement of Desire* (Pudding House Publications). She is the recipient of *CALYX's* 2014 Lois Cranston Memorial Prize, the 2012 *Princemere* Poetry Prize, and *Ruminate Magazine's* 2012 Janet B. McCabe Poetry Prize for her Pushcart Prize-nominated poem "Necessary Work," chosen by Li-Young Lee. Her poetry, nonfiction and projects have been published or are forthcoming in the *Adroit Journal, Alaska Quarterly Review, Creative Nonfiction, Radar Poetry, Ruminate Magazine, PANK, Salt Hill Journal* and *THRUSH Poetry Journal*, among others. She received her MFA from the Pennsylvania State University, and currently serves as media director for *Minerva Rising Literary Magazine* and editor of *Stitches Magazine*, which recently won a Jesse H. Neal Award.

CAREY RUSSELL received an MFA from Columbia University where she works in donor relations. Her award-winning work has recently appeared or is forthcoming in the *Iowa Review, Tupelo, New Millennium Writings, Barnstorm*, and the *Cumberland River Review*, among others.

T.J. SANDELLA is the recipient of an Elinor Benedict Prize for Poetry (selected by Aimee Nezhukumatathil) and a William Matthews Poetry Prize (selected by Billy Collins). His work has appeared or is forthcoming in *Spoon River Poetry Review, Zone 3, Passages North, Asheville Poetry Review*, the *Tusculum Review*, and the *Fourth River*, among others. He lives with his puppy, Rufio, in Cleveland, Ohio, where he's a soapbox spokesman for the rustbelt's revitalization.

ELLIE SAWATZKY grew up in the woods of Northwestern Ontario, and now lives in Vancouver, where she is completing her MFA in creative writing at the University of British Columbia. She is a recipient of the Social Sciences and Humanities Research Council (SSHRC) grant. Two of her poems were longlisted for CBC's 2014 Canada Writes Poetry Contest, and her poetry, fiction, and nonfiction can be found in *Fugue Magazine* and the *Ubyssey*.

BRITTNEY SCOTT received her MFA from Hollins University. She is the 2012 recipient of the Joy Harjo Prize for Poetry as well as the Dorothy Sargent Rosenberg Poetry Prize. Her poems have appeared or are forthcoming in such journals as *Prairie Schooner*, the *New Republic, Narrative Magazine, Alaska Quarterly Review, North American Review, Crab Orchard Review, P oet Lore, New South,* the *Malahat Review, Water-Stone Review, Salamander, Notre Dame Review, Confrontation,* and the *Journal.* Her fiction has appeared in *Quarter After Eight.* She teaches creative writing to adults, Girl Scouts, and high-risk youth at Richmond's Visual Arts Center.

MATT SUMPTER's poems have appeared or are forthcoming in the *New Yorker,* the *New Republic, Boulevard, Ninth Letter,* and *32 Poems,* and also received the *Crab Orchard Review* Special Issues Feature Award. He is currently enrolled in the creative writing PhD program at Binghamton University.

TALIN TAHAJIAN grew up near Boston. Her poetry has recently appeared in *PANK, Word Riot, DIAGRAM, Hobart, Washington Square Review,* and on *Verse Daily.* She was a finalist for the 2014 Indiana Review Poetry Prize, and serves as a poetry editor for the *Adroit Journal.* She is currently an 18-year-old undergraduate student at the University of Cambridge, where she studies English literature and attempts to assimilate.

GABRIELLA R. TALLMADGE holds an MFA from the University of North Carolina Wilmington. A finalist for the 2014 Greg Grummer Poetry Award, her work has also received a Tennessee Williams Scholarship in Poetry from the Sewanee Writers' Conference. Her poems are published or forthcoming in *Passages North, Phoebe, Devil's Lake,* the *Collagist,* the *Journal,* and others. Gabriella can be found in California and on Twitter @GRTallmadge.

A winner of a 2014 Pushcart Prize, OCEAN VUONG has received fellowships and awards from Kundiman, Poets House, Civitella Ranieri Foundation (Italy), the Elizabeth George Foundation, the Academy Of American Poets, and the Saltonstall Foundation for the Arts. His poems appear in *Poetry,* the *Nation, Boston Review, Beloit Poetry Journal, Guernica, TriQuarterly* and *American Poetry Review,* which awarded him the 2012 Stanley Kunitz Prize for Younger Poets. He lives in Queens, New York.

ANNA ROSE WELCH is a violinist and editor in Erie, Pennsylvania. She holds an MFA from Bowling Green State University. Her work has appeared or is forthcoming in *Barrow Street, Crab Orchard Review, Guernica,* the *Journal, Tupelo Quarterly,* the *Adroit Journal,* and other journals. Her first manuscript has been shortlisted for book prizes from OSU Press, the *Crab Orchard Review* Series in Poetry, and Tupelo Press.

LISA WELLS is a poet and essayist from Portland, Oregon. Her work has appeared or is forthcoming in the *Believer, Third Coast,* the *Rumpus, Ecotone, Southern Humanities Review, Hazlitt,* and others. She's the author of the chapbook *BEAST* (Bedouin, 2012) and a book of essays, *Yeah. No. Totally.* (Perfect Day, 2011). She has an MFA in poetry from the Iowa Writers' Workshop and currently teaches creative writing at the University of Iowa.

PHILLIP B. WILLIAMS is a Chicago, Illinois native. He is the author of the chapbooks *Bruised Gospels* (Arts in Bloom Inc., 2011) and *Burn* (YesYes Books, 2013), and his first full-length book, *Thief in the Interior* (Alice James Books, 2016). He is a Cave Canem graduate and received scholarships from Bread Loaf Writers' Conference and a 2013 Ruth Lilly Fellowship. His work has appeared or is forthcoming in *Anti-, Callaloo, Kenyon Review Online, Poetry,* the *Southern Review, West Branch* and others. Phillip received his MFA in writing at Washington University in St. Louis. He is the poetry editor of the online journal *Vinyl Poetry.*

JEREMY WINDHAM is currently an undergraduate student earning his BFA in creative writing at Stephen F. Austin State University where he also studies literature, music, and violin performance. His poetry can be found in the *Blue Route, Psaltery and Lyre, Steam Ticket Review,* the *Lake, Diverse Voices Quarterly,* the *Portland Review, Cider Press Review, Borderlands: Texas Poetry Review,* and is soon to appear in *Rainy Day Magazine, Southern Humanities Review,* and *Spillway.*

Acknowledgments

Nico Alvarado's "Tim Riggins Speaks of Waterfalls" was previously published in *Gulf Coast*.

Linda Blaskey's "Looking West Toward the Ozarks" was previously published in *Mojave River Review*.

Chuck Carlise's "I Can Tell You a Story" is forthcoming in *Third Coast*.

Anders Carlson-Wee's "Icefisher" was previously published in the *Pinch*.

Noel Crook's "Notes from a Salt Flat Prisoner" was previously published in *Smartish Pace*.

Benjamin Goldberg's "The Gospel According to Rust" was previously published in *Grist: The Journal for Writers*.

Miriam Bird Greenberg's "Shortness of Breath" was previously published in the *Paris-American*.

Richie Hofmann's "After" was previously published in *Ploughshares*.

Wayne Johns's "Delirium" was previously published in *New England Review*.

Andrea Jurjević's "For Yugoslavia's More Fortunate Ones" was previously published in *Verse Wisconsin*.

Corey Miller's "Willow Lake Mine" was previously published in *Narrative*.

Jenny Molberg's "Marvels of the Invisible" was previously published in *North American Review*.

Rachel Morgenstern-Clarren's "The Civil War Photographer" was previously published in *Jet Fuel Review*.

Jacques J. Rancourt's "Open Shed" was previously published in *ZYZZYVA*.

Erin Rodoni's "Two Nights in Room Nineteen" was previously published in *Verse Wisconsin*.

Carey Russell's "Mackerel" was previously published in the *Cumberland River Review*.

T.J. Sandella's "Kayaking, Early Morning" was previously published in *Zone 3*.

Gabriella R. Tallmadge's "Marriage An Animal Language" was previously published in *Crazyhorse*.

Ocean Vuong's "Anaphora As Coping Mechanism" was previously published in *Southern Indiana Review*.

Phillip B. Williams's "Do-Rag" was previously published in *Poetry*.

Jeremy Windham's "After the Funeral" was previously published in the *Lake*.

Participating Magazines

32 Poems
32poems.com

AGNI Magazine
bu.edu/agni

Anti-
anti-poetry.com

Antioch Review
antiochreview.org

Apple Valley Review
applevalleyreview.com

apt
howapt.com

Arsenic Lobster Poetry Journal
arseniclobster.magere.com

Asheville Poetry Review
ashevillepoetryreview.com

Assaracus
siblingrivalrypress.com/assaracus

B O D Y
bodyliterature.com

Bamboo Ridge: Journal of Hawaii Literature and Arts
bambooridge.com

Bellevue Literary Review
blr.med.nyu.edu

Beloit Poetry Journal
bpj.org

Birmingham Poetry Review
birminghampoetryreview.org

Boston Review
bostonreview.net

Cave Wall
cavewallpress.com

Cerise Press
cerisepress.com

Conte
conteonline.net

Crazyhorse
crazyhorse.cofc.edu

Cumberland River Review
crr.trevecca.edu

Dappled Things
dappledthings.org

EVENT
eventmagazine.ca

Fjords Review
fjordsreview.com

Flycatcher
flycatcherjournal.org

Guernica Magazine
guernicamag.com

*Gulf Coast: A Journal of Literature
and Fine Arts*
gulfcoastmag.org

H.O.W. Journal
howjournal.com

Hamilton Arts & Letters
HALmagazine.com

Harvard Review
harvardreview.org

Hayden's Ferry Review
haydensferryreview.org

Image
imagejournal.org

inter|rupture
interrupture.com

Juked
juked.com

Lunch Ticket
lunchticket.org

*Memorious: A Journal for New
Verse & Fiction*
memorious.org

Menacing Hedge
menacinghedge.com

Michigan Quarterly Review
michiganquarterlyreview.com

Muzzle Magazine
muzzlemagazine.com

Naugatuck River Review
naugatuckriverreview.com

New England Review
nereview.com

Nimrod International Journal
utulsa.edu/nimrod

Pilgrimage Magazine
pilgrimagepress.org

Pinwheel
pinwheeljournal.com

Pleiades: A Journal of New Writing
ucmo.edu/pleiades

Ploughshares
pshares.org

*PLUME: A Journal of
Contemporary Poetry*
plumepoetry.com

poetry international
poetryinternational.sdsu.edu

Prairie Schooner
prairieschooner.unl.edu

Raleigh Review
raleighreview.org

Rattle
rattle.com

River Styx
riverstyx.org

Room Magazine
roommagazine.com

Salamander
salamandermag.org

SALMAGUNDI
salmagundimagazine.tumblr.com

Skydeer Helpking
skydeer.info

Smartish Pace
smartishpace.com

Southern Humanities Review
cla.auburn.edu/shr

Southern Indiana Review
usi.edu/sir

Southwest Review
smu.edu/southwestreview

Spillway
spillway.org

St. Petersburg Review
stpetersburgreview.com

Stirring: A Literary Collection
sundresspublications.com/stirring

Subtropics
english.ufl.edu/subtropics

Sugar House Review
SugarHouseReview.com

Swarm
swarmlit.com

The *Adroit Journal*
theadroitjournal.org

The *Believer*
believermag.com

The *Bitter Oleander*
bitteroleander.com

The *Boiler*
theboilerjournal.com

The *Cincinnati Review*
cincinnatireview.com

The *Collagist*
thecollagist.com

The *Common*
thecommononline.org

The *Iowa Review*
iowareview.org

The *Journal*
thejournalmag.org

The *Lascaux Review*
lascauxreview.com

The *Normal School*
thenormalschool.com

The *Paris-American*
theparisamerican.com

The *Southeast Review*
southeastreview.org

The *Southern Review*
thesouthernreview.org

The *Tusculum Review*
tusculum.edu/tusculumreview

Thrush Poetry Journal
thrushpoetryjournal.com

Toe Good Poetry
toegoodpoetry.com

TriQuarterly
triquarterly.org

Verse Wisconsin
versewisconsin.org

Vinyl Poetry
vinylpoetry.com

Waccamaw
waccamawjournal.com

Water-Stone Review
waterstonereview.com

Willow Springs
willowsprings.ewu.edu

Participating Writing Programs

92Y Unterberg Poetry Center
New York, NY
92y.org/WritingProgram

**Ashland University
MFA Program**
Ashland, OH
ashland.edu/mfa

**Auburn University Creative
Writing Program**
Auburn, AL
cla.auburn.edu/english

**Colorado State University MFA in
Creative Writing Program**
Fort Collins, CO
creativewriting.colostate.edu

**Converse College Low
Residency MFA**
Spartanburg, SC
converse.edu/mfa

**Drew University MFA
Program in Poetry and
Poetry in Translation**
Madison, NJ
drew.edu/graduate/academics/poetry-mfa

**Emerson College MFA
Program in Writing**
Boston, MA
emerson.edu/academics/departments/writing-literature-publishing/creative-writing

**Fresno State MFA Program in
Creative Writing**
Fresno, CA
fresnostate.edu/artshum/english/graduate/mfa

FSU Creative Writing Program
Tallahassee, FL
english.fsu.edu/crw

George Mason University Creative Writing Program
Fairfax, VA
creativewriting.gmu.edu

Helen Zell Writers' Program, University of Michigan
Ann Arbor, MI
lsa.umich.edu/writers

Hollins University: Jackson Center for Creative Writing
Roanoke, VA
hollins.edu/jacksoncenter

Hunter College MFA Program in Creative Writing
New York, NY
hunter.cuny.edu/creativewriting

Iowa State University MFA in Creative Writing and Environment
Ames, IA
engl.iastate.edu/creative-writing/
mfa-program-in-creative-writing-and-environment

Johns Hopkins University Advanced Academic Programs
Baltimore, MD
advanced.jhu.edu

Johns Hopkins University MFA in Fiction and Poetry
Baltimore, MD
writingseminars.jhu.edu/graduate

Kansas State University Master of Arts in English Program in Creative Writing
Manhattan, KS
k-state.edu/english/programs/cw

McNeese State University
Lake Charles, LA
mfa.mcneese.edu

Michener Center for Writers, University of Texas at Austin
Austin, TX
utexas.edu/academic/mcw

Minnesota State University Mankato MFA Program in Creative Writing
Mankato, MN
english.mnsu.edu/cw/cwmfa.htm

NC State–Raleigh MFA in Creative Writing
Raleigh, NC
english.chass.ncsu.edu/graduate/mfa

New Mexico State University MFA Program in Creative Writing
Las Cruces, NM
english.nmsu.edu/mfa

New School Writing Program
New York, NY
newschool.edu/public-engagement/mfa-creative-writing

Northwestern University MA and MFA in Creative Writing Program
Evanston, IL
scs.northwestern.edu/program-areas/graduate/creative-writing

NYU Creative Writing Program
New York, NY
cwp.as.nyu.edu

Ohio University MA and PhD in Creative Writing
Columbus, OH
english.ohiou.edu/cw

Pacific University MFA in Writing Program
Forest Grove, OR
pacificu.edu/as/mfa

Program for Writers at the University of Illinois at Chicago
Chicago, IL
engl.uic.edu/CW

San Diego State University MFA in Creative Writing
San Diego, CA
mfa.sdsu.edu

Sarah Lawrence College MFA Program in Writing
Bronxville, NY
slc.edu/writing-mfa

Texas Tech University Department of English
Lubbock, TX
english.ttu.edu

The Arkansas Programs in Creative Writing and Translation
Fayetteville, AR
mfa.uark.edu

The Creative Writing Program at the University of Connecticut
Storrs, CT
creativewriting.uconn.edu

The Creative Writing Programs at Hamline University
St. Paul, MN
hamline.edu/cwp

The University of Alabama Program in Creative Writing
Tuscaloosa, AL
english.ua.edu/grad/cw

The University of Mississippi
University, MS
mfaenglish.olemiss.edu

University of British Columbia Creative Writing Program
Vancouver, BC
creativewriting.ubc.ca

University of Florida, MFA@FLA
Gainesville, FL
web.english.ufl.edu/crw

University of Idaho MFA Program
Moscow, ID
uidaho.edu/class/english/graduate/mfaincreativewriting

University of Massachusetts MFA for Poets and Writers
Amherst, MA
umass.edu/english/MFA_home.htm

University of Massachusetts–Boston MFA Program
Boston, MA
umb.edu/academics/cla/english/grad/mfa

University of Missouri - St. Louis MFA Program
St. Louis, MO
umsl.edu/~mfa

University of Missouri PhD Program in English Literature and Creative Writing
Columbia, MO
english.missouri.edu/creative-writing.html

University of North Dakota
Grand Forks, ND
arts-sciences.und.edu/english/graduate

University of North Texas Graduate Creative Writing Program
Denton, TX
english.unt.edu/creative-writing

University of Notre Dame Creative Writing Program
Notre Dame, IN
english.nd.edu/creative-writing

University of South Carolina MFA Program
Columbia, SC
artsandsciences.sc.edu/engl/grad/mfa

University of South Florida, Master of Fine Arts in Creative Writing
Tampa, FL
english.usf.edu/graduate/concentrations/cw/degrees

University of Tennessee Knoxville Creative Writing Program
Knoxville, TN
creativewriting.utk.edu

University of Wyoming MFA Program
Laramie, WY
uwyo.edu/creativewriting

Vermont College of Fine Arts
Montpelier, VT
vcfa.edu

Virginia Tech MFA Program
Blacksburg, VA
graduate.english.vt.edu/MFA

West Virginia University MFA Program in Creative Writing
Morgantown, WV
creativewriting.wvu.edu

Western Michigan University Creative Writing Program
Kalamazoo, MI
wmich.edu/english/creative-writing

Whidbey Writers Workshop MFA, a program of the Northwest Institute of Literary Arts
Whidbey Island, WA
nila.edu/mfa

DORIANNE LAUX's most recent collections are *The Book of Men* and *Facts about the Moon*, both available from W.W. Norton. She and her husband, poet Joseph Millar, moved in 2008 to Raleigh, where she teaches in and directs the MFA program at North Carolina State University. A National Book Critics' Circle Award and Lenore Marshall Poetry Prize finalist, Laux's other honors include a Pushcart Prize, three *Best American Poetry* selections, two NEA Fellowships, and a Guggenheim Fellowship. Recent poems appear in the *Oxford American, Southern Humanities Review*, and *American Poet* from the Academy of American Poets. The French translation of her second book, *What We Carry* (*Ce que nous portons*, Hélène Cardona, translator), was recently published by Editions du Cygne, Paris.

JAZZY DANZIGER is the author of *Darkroom* (University of Wisconsin Press, 2012), winner of the Brittingham Prize in Poetry, and has served as series editor for *Best New Poets* since 2011. She lives and works in St. Louis, Missouri and can be visited online at jazzydanziger.com.